Blink's Twinkling Tales

The Days of Creation

Maria Serediuc
Elisabeth Andra Oprescu

salz◇korn

www.salzkorn.at
Author: Maria Serediuc
Editor: Dorothy Lim
Illustrator: Elisabeth Andra Oprescu

BLINK'S TWINKLING TALES

The Days of Creation
Maria Serediuc & Elisabeth Andra Oprescu

ISBN 978-3-99 147-051-9

salz◇korn

Hi there,
I'm Blink,
your glowing friend,

With me, the wonders never end!
I'll tell you a tale of awe and might,
So gather 'round, children, hold on tight!

In the beginning, it is told,
God created

Light

bright and bold.

He said,

"Let there be light!"

and there was light!
Darkness fled and all was bright.

So, when you see the light's warm glow,
And all the beauty it can show,
Remember how it all began,
with **light**
created in GOD's
loving plan.

On Day 2, God said,

"Let there be sky!"

And there it was, floating up high,

A beautiful blue

expanse so wide,
Stretching out on every side.

When the sky turns bright and the day begins,
Let your happy voice sing and your heart within.

Sing
of God's
beauty

in this place,
And let your face reflect
His wonderful grace.

On Day 3, God said,
"Let the waters go away."
And **dry land** appeared,
here to stay.

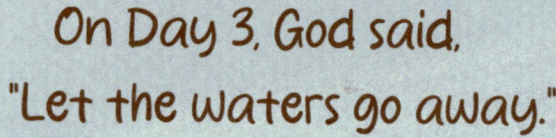

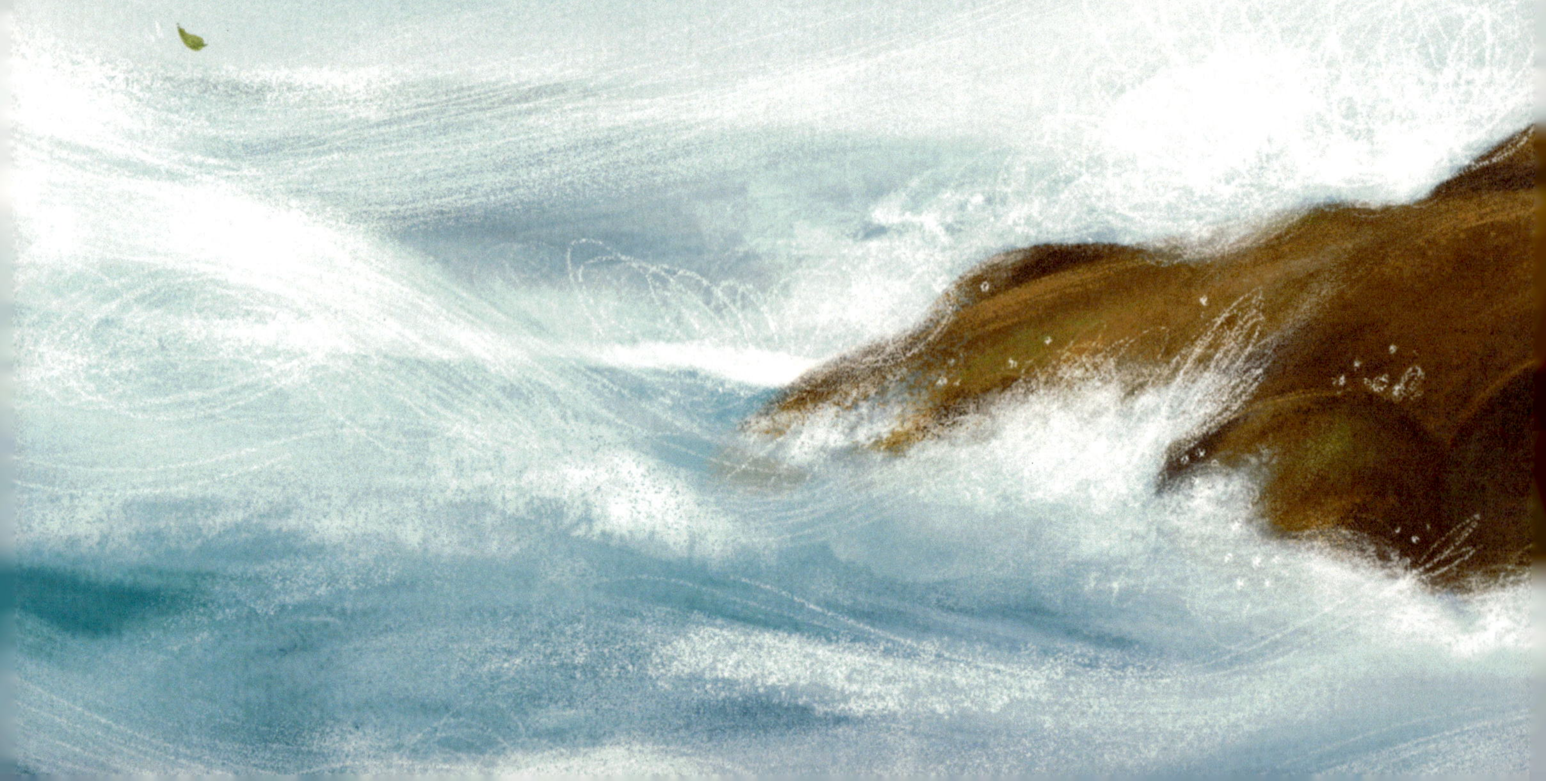

He made the grass,
the plants, and trees,
All different, with leaves
that sway in the breeze.

So, let's take care of this place we call home,
And show thanks to God for all that's grown.

Plant a tree,

smell a flower,

and **play** in the dirt,

Delight
in the garden
with a tasty dessert!

On Day 4, God said,

"Let there be

lights

To shine on the earth,
both day and night."

So, the **sun,**
moon, and **stars**
came to be,
Each in its own place, shining brilliantly.

The sun, moon, and stars remind us each day
That God is watching us in every way.

So, let's rest in peace and
sleep tight each night,
Knowing God's love is shining
like a guiding light.

On Day 5, God said,

"Let the waters be filled."

Soon creatures appeared,
there was quite a yield!

Fish and turtles, all swimming with glee
For God cares
for every creature
that lives in the sea.

Then, God made the **birds,**
they filled the air
So graceful and free, they soared everywhere.

In their carefree songs,
a message rings true,

God's love

surrounds us,
in everything we do.

On Day 6, God said, "Let there be a grand array,
A world of creatures, unique in their own way.

From the
tiniest insects
to the
mighty beasts,

Each made with a purpose,
from the west to the east."

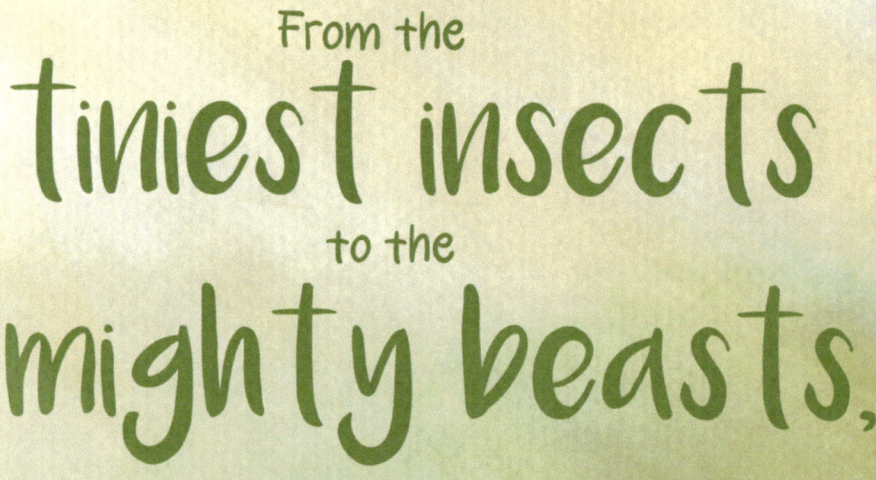

And God created
woman
and man
In His own image,
with a good plan.

He made them to
enjoy His beauty
and grace,

To dance and sing, in Love's warm embrace.

And on Day 7,

God finally
rested,

He smiled at this world He had created.

Looking at everything, big and small,
He said "It's good.
Very good."
That's all.

So, **let's be happy,**
and jump up and down,
As God gives us hugs and His love as a crown.
With kisses on our cheeks, so soft and sweet,
We know that
**God's love
is strong
and deep!**

Blink's story ...

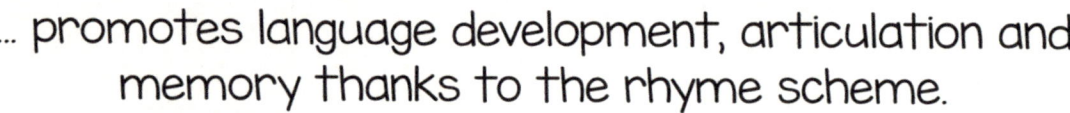

... promotes language development, articulation and memory thanks to the rhyme scheme.

... encourages us to discover God's stories together with little Blink and find applications for everyday life.

... strengthens the understanding of being beautifully created as man or woman.

Mag. Claudia Krupensky
(former Neurologist, Biology and Chemistry teacher, Missionary, experienced Children's group leader and Children's book author)

Parents are called to do something very special:
to nourish, protect and encourage the hearts of their
children, so that their unique potential can develop.

The illustrations of Blink's Twinkling Tales provide parents
the possibility to answer basic questions every toddler
has and help them to understand the way God created
this world and our bodies in an unique way and beautifully.

Together, let's be the first to teach them!

Made in the USA
Columbia, SC
05 April 2025